THE LONG WALK

ᏲᏁᏏ

OSKANA POETRY & POETICS

Jan Zwicky

The Long Walk

UNIVERSITY OF REGINA PRESS

Printed and bound in Canada by Friesens. The text of this book is printed on 100% post-consumer recycled paper with earth-friendly vegetable-based inks.

Cover design: Duncan Campbell, U of R Press
Proofreader: Kristine Douaud

The text face is Arno, designed by Robert Slimbach. The titling faces are Diotima, designed by Gudrun Zapf von Hesse, and Castellar, designed by John Peters.

Canada Council   Conseil des Arts
for the Arts   du Canada

Canada

creative
SASKATCHEWAN

Library and Archives Canada Cataloguing in Publication

Zwicky, Jan, 1955–, author
   The long walk / Jan Zwicky.

(Oskana poetry & poetics)
Poems.
Issued in print and electronic formats.
ISBN 978-0-88977-449-0 (paperback). –
ISBN 978-0-88977-450-6 (pdf)

   I. Title.

   II. Series: Oskana poetry & poetics

PS8599.W53L65 2016   C811'.54
                 C2016-903057-1
                       C2016-903058-X

10   9   8   7   6   5   4   3   2   1

UNIVERSITY OF REGINA PRESS
University of Regina
Regina, Saskatchewan
Canada S4S 0A2
TELEPHONE: (306) 585-4758
FAX: (306) 585-4699
WEB: www.uofrpress.ca
EMAIL: uofrpress@uregina.ca

The University of Regina Press acknowledges the support of the Canada Council for the Arts for our publishing program. We acknowledge the financial support of the Government of Canada. / *Nous reconnaissons l'appui financier du gouvernement du Canada.* This publication was made possible through Creative Saskatchewan's Creative Industries Production Grant Program.

for Robert Bringhurst

COURAGE

And now you know that it won't turn out as it should,
      that what you did was not enough,
            that ignorance, old evil, is enforced

and willed, and loved, that it
      is used to manufacture madness, that it is the aphrodisiac
            of power and the crutch of lassitude, you,

an ordinary heart, just functional, who knows
      that no one's chosen by the gods, the aspens
            and the blue-eyed grass have voices of their own,

what will you do,
      now that you sense the path unraveling
            beneath you?

Sky unraveling, unraveling
      the sea, the sea that still sees everywhere
            and looks at every thing —

not long. What will you do,
      you, heart, who know the gods don't flee,
            that they can only be denied.

Who guess their vengeance.

It has been a long hill, heart.
      But now the view is good.
            Or don't you still believe

the one sin is refusal, and refusal to keep seeking
        when refused?
                        Come, step closer to the edge, then.

You must look, heart. You must look.

CONTENTS

I

for NW 29-57-08 W5 & SW 32-57-08 W5

To set out west, into the windbreak's gap,
and through the memory of the poplars roaring on the night
your father died, the memory of the bench, not house,
he built high in their branches — you could look out
to the first rise of the foothills — and the tunnels
in the caraganas underneath, dog-
haunted, their dry and scented shade.
And the tunnels in the drifts that built up in their lee
— six feet deep one winter — your mitts ice-clotted and the light
that cut slits where your eyes once were.
Out to the slow roll down the river's slope, the barley green
as silk the year it came up to your chin, alfalfa
later, and the dandelions in the three-year drought.
Past the septic outflow where we threw the brush and burnt it
in the winter dark, down through the draw, its aspens silver
in the cold spring rain. The rain.
The beavers and the beaver slides, the wreckage
of the bottom land the other side: flood-tattered willows
and their drapes of matted grass. Stumbling in the weeds,
the bedstraw and the roses, or the goldenrod, the felled logs
random and invisible. That open winter, minus forty, ice fans
stacked like mushrooms in the crystal fog, the water's voice
still trickling in the shallows, bubbles slipping eel-like
under ice. The fallen log you sat on
when you knew that it would end. The hay bale
in whose shade you lay as it began. The red-tail and the white-tailed
      buck,
the explosion of the sunset at the line fence, and the mane of hail
above the muskeg; the thunderheads, their silence
in the shining light. There, at the northwest corner, wild strawberries

most years and the ancient culvert where we found
the porcupine. Beyond the fence,
the tracks, the built-up rail bed and the load of gravel once
with tiny garnets in the soft black schist. The willow mist
that settled August evenings after rain. How you paced
the northwest field three times with your sister,
making her believe. The decade that she didn't speak to you.
There, buttercups. And blue-eyed grass.
And down the lane, then, to the barn, its emptiness:
the corral gone, and the lean-to, and the mud,
the root cellar and the pig barn, and the grey board fence.
Your mother's mare, dead in the draw, her bloodshot eye.
Barbed wire down the middle of the old track to the ford,
the track itself slumped riverwards, young balsam poplar saplings
        thickening,
and thistles where the lease cows overgrazed.
Where the ford was, the banks
steep, foreign. Wild raspberries, but few. The sharp thump
of the wagon on the round white stones, the John Deere
snorting up the far side. The six-foot wooden fork, tipped high
along the haystack, leaping off
on to the sloping thatch. Or stacking square bales on the stoneboat,
piling them in stooks. That evening when your gelding
felt the desert in his genes and flew with you across the stubble
in the low blue light. Coming down again by bottom land
towards the river, crossing on a beaver dam — the little meadow
and the little neck of land the river hasn't cut through, honeypails
of saskatoons some summers, and the anthills crowding down
        the slope,
small dun volcanoes. Up above the barn again, but east of it,
the walk on into town, except why would you go.

Or there, back to the house, except
why would you go.
                    To go through, then —
wild rose scent
on the air, or orange hips
in the smoke-brown grass. When you lose a limb,
it's said, you see but don't believe. Geese
overhead, crows scattering before a northern front, the bell
of courting chickadees some windless
February afternoon. The body
knows before the mind collects itself: what held you
is what held you up, at every step,
                              to set out then
into the walk that keeps on walking. Coming home
without a roof.

for Don McKay

It was early June, and though the trail led high,
we thought the week of record heat made it
worth chancing. We'd had luck: gas stations
open late, fresh fruit at the diner in Leduc. And then,
strolling the vacant campground at the turnoff,
we'd found a swollen stream that ran
like liquid ice and numbed our hands so thoroughly we lay
along the footbridge — two thick planks —
and stroked the Dolly Varden trout that gathered,
shadowy, intent, beneath it. Our guidebook
said the trail stuck with the stream
right to its source, a tarn another hour's hike
above the pass. We decided: if the weather held,
we'd leave at 6:00 and try to make
the top. It did; and as we climbed,
our luck held, too: the woods completely clear
to start, and higher up, linked meadows
open to the sun. Always the stream. It wasn't
until mid-afternoon the trail turned sharply back
around the long toe of a ridge and we
hit snow: a slope of trees, steep in the lee, the stream
shallowed, splintering among them. In places,
it was three feet deep, in places
cataracted panes of ice, and water gushing everywhere,
we had to shout and still could not be heard, the light
cartwheeling off the snow, our eyes
gasping for purchase in the swaths of deep
spruce shade, the tessellated mass of rock and
deadfall, the path, the slope, a tumbling ecstatic
roar, sun, shadow, our hearts leaping

as we plunged upwards,
drenched and blind.

                    That afternoon, there,
thrown against the tangled white,
we were our best.
There we are still.

The house no house I'd known,
tall, narrow, with a steep exterior stair,
and at the bottom, at the road's edge,

my grandmother — or, no — or, yes — my mother's
grandmother, the dark paint on the shingles
sombre, hard, like nothing

in the pencil drawing that I'd stared at hours as a child:
a woman, young, a basket full of flowers on her arm,
she's walking through a gate that opens on a road —

and yet, that drawing. Made by my mother's
grandmother. Why her, there,
in that dream? — grandmother both of me and of

my mother, who now from her single room
is looking out into the black-knot-covered branches
of an ancient May-day tree. Or do I mean

who was the person that had walked to meet her
down the long lane of my childhood,
mud and gravel, grass barely showing in the verge, it was

spring, the contours of the fields
those I grew up with but the fields themselves
too distant, and the west one a plantation

that it never could have been: saplings, rows of them,
stiff, pink with bloom, the air like glass
before or after rain.

I thought I was with others, but I was alone
when I crossed into my new life: all dissolution
was within. That lie — what had I said,
or failed to say — the shock of it — I thought,
then, it was one of them, I thought the reason
was his beauty, or his genius; or, I thought,
it was because of her, the accidental past;
I thought: because she'd died. But it was
nothing I could think, it was
some physics of the body, atoms, cells,
which opened in the dark like flowers on an apple tree,
like stars, testifying. They were
the point of entry, they belonged, first,
to the earth. It was like that. Brute. Exquisite.
My legs kept moving, we were on our way
downslope, the sudden, steep internal silence,
numb, bewildering, the sense
a second soul was lifting, splitting from my own.
You who read this, you, most conscious
and most self-aware: at any moment,
in the far reach of the deepest, most unhurried solitude,
clear-eyed, near the end, the valley
close, I'd glimpsed it — even there,
and blind, you could be taken.
Chaos, terror, the shrapnel I'd become, the wreckage
fountaining, erupting through the silence,
the emptiness of where I'd been. —
Or not. That other emptiness, what would have been
a lie if it were not the truth.
How bright the sun was, how thoughtlessly
we'd opened to its warmth,

the first Spring Azure heart-stopping on the mat
of winter scurf. Don't tell me that I knew.
Don't tell me that I didn't.
I was alive,
one step to the next, worlds ending.

SECURING THE HOUSE

What is it we are trying
to achieve? That we will learn
before we die to make
our leaving orderly? Imagine

turning down the heat
and walking out, not even
locking up, imagine
coming back weeks later. Ah,

the list of failures: unpaid bills,
the missing jewellery, plant leaves
browning on the window sills.

And the dust. What of the dust?

You come from the same direction that
they did: the misinformed,
the would-be heroes, unfirst
European sons who knew
how much a pickaxe weighed, the ones
who didn't. A hundred years later
and it's morning still, sun at your back: you're driving
down the highway, rich and female, in your unimaginable
car.

Two, three, half a dozen
elevators at each siding once. Sometimes the same red
as the boxcars, more often white, and the one
your mother's generosity has helped preserve, the one
that's cresting the horizon, there, in the right-hand corner of your
    windscreen
is a faded grayish-green. Alberta Wheat Pool, Pioneer,
Searle, UGG. Thousands of them
in the middle decades of the century. Last count
in Alberta, 169.
        2000,
the year they started raising funds to save it,
they made a postcard, got a grant to pay a kid
to sit all summer at the office desk in case of tourists.
There were none.

A memory of its dimness (brilliant squares
of August sunshine that the wagon entered from
and drove back into): shafts
and levers creaking: an immense
Cartesian animal. Your mom says it was 1999

they closed all three. And then tore down
the other two. Weeds, and the windows
broken, even the little one five stories up.
The shock wave of that dream of ownership, that failure
of connection whose real name
we refuse

> *still passing through,*
> *still passing through,*
> *violence descending*
> *with the northern twilight,*
> *Saturday night*
> *and nothing to do.*

That craziness. Its disordering
of hope. It deranged us all,
three generations, sometimes four: the picket fence,
the pasture and its spotted cows, abstracted finally
to something more like cold hard cash. —For? Well,
maybe that vacation, we could get away, or get
an RV or an iPad. Get a wall-sized
LCD.

Weeds again now. Frost fence. The windows on the tower
boarded up. A small rock through the bottom left-hand
pane beside the office door, stopped by the sheet of plexiglass
inside. A hundred years, and it's still
August, sky the dusky blue that means
dry heat.

> *Edward Hopper, what's to tell.*
> *Everything's just fine here,*
> *ordinary as hell.*

Main Street. Vacant. Clean. The Dollar Store
closed up, the chiropractor and the flower shop. You drive
to Whitecourt now, or buy online. The Co-op and the Rexall
still in business, but the parking lot unused —
two half-tons and a single car perched at the curb.
Clean inside, too: linoleum a lustrous, dark and
unmarked forest green.

But she was right, my mom, to try to save
the elevator. Loyalty
isn't clinging, it's a way
to know. Long love, its fragile afterlife:
details that we can't forget.
What's coming
won't be human if it has
no ghost.

II

Wind hurls itself through the streets
on some terrible mission. Best not

to look. Down in the basement,
it's cool; you can't hear the glass.

Late nights in the boiler room of the spirit,
our bad conscience like that cough

we won't take to the doctor.
Floors of locked hallways above us.

We could automate, you know. No need
for solitaire. Imagine

the freedom: when the weather's good enough,
picnics in the scorched weeds, they'll

rope off the jellyfish at the beach.
We'll stride from the waves,

plastic flecking our hair
like confetti.

It arrives. The far dream
        that terrified us — that put the steel
in our forearms, and we woke each morning
        to its distant shuddering —

is far no more. Heavy-limbed, it sprawls
        across the daylight, brushes back
the damp hair from our foreheads, stares
        and laughs. And the axle of our will

is seized, the wheel splintered, an engine
        that does not, does not
turn, and when we go below decks, find
        it is missing, a hollow, a dark sift

of emptiness, and the ferry is slammed
        against its moorings, helpless, the contagion spreading,
and the one who knows, the one who has been readied,
        is absent from the table.

Near is the hard grief, the grief
        from the pit, whose hands shake, which cannot find
the knife, which cannot stand, or kneel, or lie,
        the grief that is tearless, that gags.

The clearcut, the dead zone, the gas-contaminated
        well, the salt earth, the foreign
investment protection, the child soldier,
        the rape, the spin, the addiction

to speed, the saving of labour, the image,
      the image, the image, the image,
the genetic modification, the electromagnetic
      field, the sense of entitlement, greed. The present

is thick-lipped and stunned; it sweats. The voice
      of the century is a wild clanking, a loose stink that lifts
and settles in our mouths. Did you raise your hand? Did you
      say something? Louder. Louder.

for Susan Stewart

How soon the body molds itself
around the new. Our sure steps
to the hotel bathroom in the middle of the night,
its bleakness already settling in the bones.

And the soul, a loose cloak wrapped around the shoulders,
going where the body goes,
drooping as the shoulders droop. The grime
around the neck. The tattered hem.

Culture is the river of us: the glaciers
of love, the rocks of hunger and intelligence,
the gravity of power, gadgetry and greed.
No one can resist. Ask the rain.

The river tumbles out
into the space beyond the cliff.
Sometimes in the thunder of the updraft,
a cloak, spreading like a sail.

Desire, you who lift us each morning,
      rough as the disc of the sun,
you who bind us, who drag us half senseless
      through the gift of our pain,

who leap without thought, who climb
      with the climber who seizes the air
in the fists of his lungs, drinking
      the light with the lungs of his eyes,

tell me: even the dead do not know,
      even those who are ashes and sleeping now
under the lake, their extravagance
      earns them no answer.

You, who live high in the mountains,
      where being itself empties down like the falls,
sometimes in tumult, here glassy with weight, its pour
      as though motionless: see

how the air, the melodious air,
      fills the clearing: floating the grass
and the palm-bright leaves. Their breathing
      like sleep, and the year that completes itself in them.

If I go down on my knees, if I go down
      in the burnt yellow grass, in the somnolent leaves,
what will this serve? No appeal,
      no assuaging the centuries,

the droughts and the floods, the poisoned and vanished
      that pile up and stagger against the horizon.
The sick sky won't swallow me, its sick heat
      won't melt the scab of my fear.

The souls of the alders, the souls of the firs,
      the souls of the red-bellied newts and
the golden-crowned kinglets, the uncountable souls of the grasses,
      making one soul, one bending

at dawn. Where will my soul go
      when it can't walk among them?
When the earth I have loved turns its back
      and closes its eyes.

I will lie down, then, in the wreckage of meaning.
      In the rot of the forest, the rot of the wind.
I will lie down in the shouting and silence,
      the dust of you filling my mouth.

The Old Dream

A room — a space — so large perhaps
it had no ceiling. And past the threshold,
through the open door, a landscape
falling into twilight — pink and mauve, a haze
of frost. I was
behind you, had been searching, urgent; you
were on your way
to meet me, stepping through that doorway, hair
silver in the silver light. I called.
You turned. And in your eyes

I saw you would refuse. But then,
a second later, knew instead
that it was I who had said no.

The grief stood in me like a knife.
And in that instant, like a fairy tale,
the floor, your hand, shoes, clothes, the light, the doorframe,
shed their surfaces. I saw
things as they are.

But still
I could not see myself.

Terminal

Featureless, the sky, dark gray.
The heavy light before a storm.
The elevators, too, dark, purplish,
their tiered, unfathomable complex
stretched for miles around the lake.
Completely empty. Nothing
to be done. The other animals
all fled.

My footsteps hollow
on the walkways.
The panes of sightless glass
like metal in the rising wind.

Night Farm

This time, you visit in the middle of the day.
Outside, rare sunshine; the unruffled pond
deep in its January dream.

But you come again as you were, as you must
still be, in the night: the aspens
like a rank of disused swords,
hoar on the pebbles of the lane,
receding snowlight in the fields.
Dreamless.

The way we are
when we believe we are no longer loved.

Leaving

She is walking away, she is
walking away. You are furious.
Her husband is trying not to cry. He is
crying. No one understands,
not her children, not her mother, her sister
does not exist.

You are walking away, you are
walking away. Who are you,
furious with yourself,
who is trying not to cry.
Who is crying.

Earlier each day comes the light
        and our appetite, the terror that we are,
                shines darkly in every living thing.

The drought intensifies, its yammer
        wilder, more dimensionless: no one
                is listening and everything

is listened to: each keystroke, every flutter
        in the grid. Our confected optimism and
                our medicated sleep.

What is it that we have not seen
        and think we can in this way see
                — our innocence? the cartoon

of our harmlessness? how hard we tried?
        Invisible, the benediction of the alders,
                their sprightly shade.

In the shallows, thought
        unfurls itself: dazed, sunburnt,
                querulous. What does it want?

Fat. Sugar. The world's neck
        motionless beneath its foot. It wants
                to understand. But everywhere

the glare of meaning's absence.
        Gunfire's distant thud and clack.
                The rain that never comes.

> *... until the opening of* CFB *Suffield in 1971, Camp*
> *Gagetown was the largest military training facility in*
> *Canada and the British Commonwealth of Nations.*
> —WIKIPEDIA

We're playing Casino in the living room
when a glass bursts in the kitchen.
The army is banging away again:
tiny shards in the butter, a pebble
like a doll's eye in the coffee pot.
All night the radio's been telling us

Boris Yeltsin is the hero of the hour.
"No!" he cries, "the Russian people
are the heroes of the week!" We love them
all, we love them better than we love ourselves.
The army is banging away again as Vilnius
reminds us, gently, that we
promised them HDTV when it was over.

Doors will open, heads will roll,
eras will dawn, there will be hell to pay.
It's liberty, it's solidarity, it's
the prime-time politics we've been waiting for.
The army is banging away again, and
the vacuum cleaner's working overtime: glass

like salt along the window ledge.
Now the party's over, there'll be
dancing in the streets. Troops will smile
as they retreat from Leningrad, from St. Petersburg,
as they parade this year, like every other year,

down the streets of Fredericton, New Brunswick,
just east of where, now

the army is banging away again.
It's August, it's hot, in a few days school
will start and it's time to close up
the cottage: sweep out the crumbs,
the beach sand, gather up the pine cones and
the birds' nests. Soon

those tanks will roll, flags
brilliant in the sunlight, soldiers
waving like the queen, like the girl next door,
"So long! So long!" squinting into the sun,
shielding your eyes against the glitter,
the fond safe heartache of farewell
called after the one you'll marry anyway.

III

DEPARTURE AT DAWN

Bare rooms, the echo of white light.
The moon, I think,
is a white sail of pain.

The answer isn't love or furniture,
we're always on the move.

A satellite a hundred miles up
paces its slow curve. Landscape
glides beneath it. Scars.

> *Und was für Buße willt du nun thun?*
> *Edward, Edward!*
> *Und was für Buße willt du nun thun?*

There wasn't, there wasn't, and yet there was

a land whose king was called away.
Many men went with him but he left
the best in charge: he asked his brother
to look after things.
It was summer and the sun shone, children
rough-housed in the courtyard, gulls hung stationary
in the wind above the cliffs. But in time
the young man found that he was watching
the hands of the wife of his brother
as they patched coats for the poor; he found that he listened
when her voice sent food from her kitchen
to the sick. When the smile in her eyes
touched his own, he bowed his head.
Sat late, staring into the fire.

One day she smiled and he spoke to her.
In front of them all, he asked her
to walk with him. In front of them all she agreed.
They went the main path up the hillside,
and the sun was bright on their hair.
They kept in plain view, the village could see them,
but only the wind heard the words that they said.

News came the king was returning. The queen went herself
to the rooms of his brother.
He'd vanished. The villagers said he took ship

with nothing. Sun bright on the hillside,
bright at the end of the pier. And the storm
came from nowhere. The only survivor
told how the king's brother had stood at the rail like a statue
as the ship lunged and pitched.

And the child born nine months later, none
more beautiful, the child was called
by his name. For the king had loved him so.
But she turned from the world as she grew,
never married. Stared in the night out to sea.

She did not tell what she saw then,
moonlight breaking through clouds to the water.
The gleam like a ring, spars lifting then falling,
the blind waves rolling through.

My sisters,
you who've
been in love with men:

think now
of the lover
who never had a name. The one

you never told about,
although you loved him
as no other.

Perhaps he was your brother,
or the lover of your sister.
Perhaps he was the boy

who, had your father known,
he would have killed.
Think on him now:

that boy, that man.
How you went to him,
and how he entered you.

And is he dead? Is he
married to another?
Perhaps he left

and no one heard from him
again. But if he came to you once more,
my sisters — dead,

or old, or married to another —
what would startle in your eyes?
Would it be joy,

or sorrow?
Hold the ghost inside you
to the light, my sisters,

say to him, *This is my life*
and what my life
became. Yes, what my life becomes still,

thanks to you.

NO

in memoriam Aisha Ibrahim Duhulow,
1995–2008

Because she was a woman
she'd been raped.
Because she was a woman
there was no excuse.
Because she was a woman
they dragged her to the pit.
You can hear the dull snap
as the bone breaks under flesh.

Because she is a woman
they make a nurse dig out
the shaft grave underneath
the slumped pulp of the head.
The heart still beating faintly.
It goes on.

Once there was a war.
The smoke was bad
and when it cleared, some said
that language could no longer bear
the weight of poetry.

Whose words were these?
Because they are women,
they stand in line.
One to another,
the question passes down.

MEDITATION LOOKING WEST FROM
THE BERKELEY HILLS

Then, even the work dissolves —
whatever it was. The great ships
motionless in the enormous bay,
gone the next time you look up.

And have you ever really wanted anything
except that disappearing act,
the open ocean, all horizon,
just the other side of the bridge?

Its vastness makes it comprehensible, frames
the restlessness, reduces it
to stationary shimmer. Who wouldn't
want to let go. Who wouldn't choose

those distances. They're too big
to get the mind around, too big
even for the heart. Though we try each day,
falling more and more silent.

It's love, in the end, that we learn, learning also
it isn't ours. Inexplicably, unsummoned,
the world rises to fill its own emptiness. We feel it
reaching through us — a voice, a hand,

a greenness not our own —
and are buoyed up momentarily, amazed,
before we find our feet again,
or drown.

for Warren Heiti and Tim Lilburn

You arrived at the door at last,
worn thin with love, the others, too,
translucent at the temples and the lips,
spilling up the stairs into that long room
as if it were a dream.

It was. I'd seen it. Different furniture
and there were only three of us. But
that space, that day, the mountain
back of us, and, in the dream, French windows
opening towards it, a curtain rippling in the wind.

Then the old wood table,
the hands above it, gesturing, the clear light
of the others' listening. The speech
that rose up through us had no personality,
history, but no personality,
the old grief bright in each of us, pure

trajectory of desire. And when it had enough of us,
it set us down. The others left. You looked at me
and then left, too, as though walking out into the sunshine
were a simple thing to do. In the dream,
it was our host left standing by the stairs,
but even he'd stepped out, was gone.

I was alone. All doors to the house stood open,
the way the soul stands in such moments, struck,
still vibrating. And something nameless, then,
walked past me, brushed my shoulder,
stirred the air beside my face.

Space: six-handed: whole,
unbroken. Time: the seventh hand. Time is
the arrow; asymmetrical;
the hunter with one eye.
For we grow old but don't, except in love,
grow young again. And lovers, opening their arms,
give shining birth to that which dies.

Always the skeptic.

The clean split wood on fire throws back
the summer day, the sun
love locked inside it. Isn't this
a kind of symmetry in time?
It is a gift. But not
the other hand. The ash
is leafless. What was wound unwinds,
but does not wind again.

Always the rule-bound.

No, it is the shape of space
that sings, the throat-strung vault
above the mountains, depth
and depthless, the starlit air above the stony bridge,
its resonant blue. Here,
language ceases. We glimpse, obliquely,
radiance: a kind of deathlessness
or death, whole and unbroken.
Life strives to press against it,
matchless, musical, it touches
all-directioned joy, and causeless,

without fear, as the old one said,
it is.

Always the one who must belong.

What isn't is argument. What isn't
is one-pointed will. Only in time
is mind cut by the watercourse of reasoning
and consequence. Only in time
does the cut mind make tools
of what it can no longer see
is itself. Intelligence, unlanguaged,
glimpses, skewed, oblique, a universe
in which time has its other half.

The jealous.

Music is the form of light we hear.
Language, straining to honour, to be like
that all-directioned blue
bends back on itself. It breaks
the arrow. Fearless, it sings.
For to lie in shining fragments
is better, closer to the real.
When time's shape in the mind is shattered,
truth gleams in the interstice.

Always the antagonist.

The circle, the rebirth, each year again
the leaves suffusing, the stream swelling and dappling
and the light again inside the eye
of each sexed thing: isn't this
time whole, time mirroring itself, unchanging change

becoming what it was? It is.
But not this grey one, not her
goldenness; some other dying thing is born
out of her being. Beings
held apart in language are dismantled by the very thing
whose shape gives language life: syntax
has an arrow at its heart, and the circle
is a helix, is a line.

Always the inconsolable.

And yet not so, not so completely:
mind, in memory, is still mind.
Meaning touches us, it stands before us
with a force that shocks us, each time new.
And new again, across time's distances, it flexes
everywhere unlike what can be said.

Always the one who says no prayer.

Always the righteous.
Always the one with little judgement,
and the one filled with ressentiment.
Always the professional.

And always the one who keeps open inside
that space where the god least of all
uses words.

IV

Except for the angle of the sun,
      it's just like yours.
Except the machines are larger,
      the damage is the same.
Except they're smaller,
      not quite so forlorn.

And here, too, half a century ago,
      some child waking in the violence
to what could be loved:
      a hard bright wind, the hawks,
the sky's height, and the ditches
      scabbing over with those

inextinguishable weeds. And pushed,
      or was it pulled,
beyond that love, away. So that except
      for what she buried up there
underneath the line fence,
      now it's empty of her. Just like yours.

Last night
the wind rose as the light was fading,
and the rain came, first as sheets and then as walls
of water that were slammed against the house. Trees
bellowed in the darkness, branches tearing,
crashing on the roof. But in the middle of the tumult —
faint, impossible — I suddenly heard frogsong,
waves of it, ecstatic, shimmering — a second voice
inside the storm.
                    And I remembered
that other spring: the world was ending then, too,
as I sat reading at my kitchen table, sunlight
slim among the dark leaves of the laurel hedge
outside my window.
                    It was
your letter that I read. You'd seen
a clutch of salmonberry petals, moist, you said, as tears
and colourful as candy, untouchable
as stars, snagged on a piece of alder bark,
black, in the shallows of a stream.
You told me this, and in the instant that I saw it,
I was claimed — though at the time
I thought I had been gutted, that there was nothing
I could give. I read,
and closed my eyes. And as the tears came,
as the sob or growl rose in my throat,
it opened. Who were you,
to name me so? To kiss me as you did. To tell me
what I had to love: that seeing,
through which the wind would howl,
destroying, healing my life?

She drops me off a mile away, can't bear
to look. A dusty mile — it's been too hot
for days. But the roadside ditch is full, still,
from the record snow last winter. Along it,
half-drowned aspens struggling into leaf.

He'd finally returned her call,
said it would be fine if we came out, but that
his back was bad, he hadn't
got the garden in. I didn't have the heart
to tell her what I'd seen the year before.
And now, the dead spruce in the windbreak,
the dead canes in the raspberries.
Last year's thistles five feet high.

Loyalty to what
insists on seeing this? Down by the river,
beavers have taken every tree along the flats
and up the draw north to the field.
Balsam poplars two feet through, older
than I am, older than my mother, than
the farm. Raw. Unbury-able.

As I bushwhack, stumbling up through the ravine,
there, where forty years ago the orioles would nest,
a flash of orange and black. Sudden, unbelievable,
that arterial voice.
Marsh marigolds, like startled echoes in the ooze.
The aspens coming into leaf.

We went north to the Athabasca, to the place the ferry
used to cross outside Blue Ridge. That time I was a child,
taken by my mother and my grandmother,
the day dark after rain, the air like crystal but the sky opaque,
the ferry swung out wildly in the current, yanked and shuddered, the
    cable
taut and straining. But that other afternoon, there was sun,
late summer, and a new bridge, swallows
packing mud up to their tenements, a long unbroken line of them
under the railings either side. We crossed
and took the turn a half mile on and bumped back
through the trees towards the north bank. Beer cans,
condoms, scattered blackened sticks. The warm light, northern, slanting,
filtered through the poplars. Chickadees and kinglets. Two cottonwoods
had grown huge, they'd become great trees: six feet around and one
at least a hundred high. Rare in Alberta. They made me
think of Europe, and that made me think
of how I'd thought of Europe as a child: a place of spaciousness
and shade, of nuance without malice, justice without carnage,
that there might be peace and wit and ease, how I'd wanted
what I'd never seen, what I had no word for,
style. And I glimpsed the poverty of how I'd lived,
how everyone I'd known had lived. But what I see now
is how deadly that wish was, not to be lost. Those cottonwoods,
it was twenty years ago, there've been bad floods, not old
if they'd been oaks but still, the fierce inconsequence
of beauty. That hard tug underneath the breastbone as we're
    swung out
in the current, the cutbank steep above us, pocked with swallow holes,
the sharp edge of the mountain air, shadows
blurring, deepening.

THE LAST ADAGIO

after Haydn String Quartet in C, Opus 54 No. 2: Finale

Shaken, tense, your hands blunt
with clenching the wheel, the sudden
warmth and noise, "You made it!", but they're not
the ones you were expecting, others,
stranded by the storm, the ferries down, your friends
still in another city, and the evening
suddenly impossible, your conversation
a shambles, haunted by that slush-choked road,
the darkness, snow thickening in your headlights, you can't
stay here, you don't know
these people, you will have
to go back, you will have to go

without explanation, the road
unreadable now, no tracks, the heater roaring,
wipers useless in the ice, and the car
in the sleet, in the dark, spinning out
above the cutbank, the long arc we know already
for it is the soul's, how it rises from us
like scent on a summer's evening, what is deep
climbing steadily, breaking the surface
like grief, like love, a tenderness
we can't imagine but still recognize, opening
and opening its hands.

At the end, far into the afternoon,
I'd walk the same trail, when I could,
up to the ridge. For often then,
but only at that time of day, there would be
sun. The creeks still overflowing and the path
still slick, but what gushed
among the rocks and deadfall was alight,
the droplets flashing in the firs — gold, emerald,
rose — their sharp glint echoed
in the polished tangle of the overgrown salal.

And I saw that it was true,
what you had taught me: beauty
insists: it is connexion
with the real. Even on the days I couldn't tell my sorrow
from the world's: the sudden calm
that was your touch, how I was trued
inside your glance. The long and level shaft of light
at day's end, reaching from the planet's edge
beneath its lid of cloud. That clarity.
Brief brightness on the earth.

Was there a time I did not know you? The continents
had other names and shapes, perhaps; the days
before the feather was invented; before
the sea was blue. Even then

the muscles of your shoulders could not
lift the world. Though
I think you tried: this scar, here; the long bruise
you never talk about

that never fades. How beautiful
you must have been then, bronze and flashing,
for how beautiful you are: though now
the birds are falling from the sky, the terrifying rain

has washed the slope away. This back of yours,
what it still bears. You are
the one I've always walked towards, the one I've sensed
as salt, as wind, as answer. Now, at last, you turn from me,

the soft whuff of your sleeping self,
the white wisps of your hair like tufts of silk,
like so much that I love:
strewn, fragile, mortal, gleaming.

It is finished. The golden toad,
the gold-edged gem, silver hair moss
and the sapphire-bellied hummingbird.

It is finished. Rainbow mussels
and the yellow-crested cockatoo,
aurora trout and Taylor's checkerspot.
The blue whale. The magenta petrel, and the
grey-shanked douc. It's finished
for the copper redhorse, purple twayblade,
for spotted wintergreen. The red knot.

Also for the geometric tortoise
and the five-lined skink, the heart-leaved plantain
and the oval pigtoe. Forked three-awned grass.

It is finished. The piping plover,
Kirtland's warbler, vesper sparrows
and horned larks. Finished for the
Western screech-owl and the
yellow-breasted chat.

Finished for the oldest beings on the planet:
pines, the bristlecones. Also the whitebarks.

Dense blazing star. It's finished.
Thread-leaved sundew and
the half-moon hairstreak.

Hoary mountain mint.
Frosted glass-whiskers.
The mottled duskywing.

The Table Mountain ghost frog.

Immeasurable thanks:
it got here.
Your guess was right, it
took a beating.
But the gist's intact.
You'll understand me
when I say our situation
is uncertain.
We'll do our best
to send it on.
Expect us soon.

Finally the death's-door cases had been
cleared: the heart attack, the stroke, the overdose, the guy
who had a pillowcase stuffed up his nose and blood
still pouring down his face. It was just
the old guy in the wheelchair and his son
and me. CNN on the flatscreen in the corner.
They were glad to see the back of Harper
but they weren't keen on another
Democratic president. The old guy
said he did hydraulics for the logging industry,
one piece in particular — (I couldn't catch it, yarders?) —
installed them now on trucks. "Can't have
fourteen, fifteen guys coolin their heels up
Toba Inlet while they fly it into Campbell
to be fixed." The doctor came into
the waiting room, sat down beside me, jolly,
young: "The good news is you don't need surgery!
But see," he held an iPad up, "just there:
you broke the fibula. I could splint it,
but you'll need to ice six times a day this week.
You'd have to wrap it up each time. You'd be better
in an aircast. Oh." He looked up at the clock. "Except
the place you'd get one's closed." I thought
about another ferry trip, the bad storms
ripping up the strait day after day, the cancelled
sailings and the way my foot kept swelling.
"I'm from Quadra," I began, "I'll take —"
"Phone Joe's," the old guy said. "He'll have em."
"Joe's?" the doctor said. "Joe's. Up on Merecroft."
Unsure, the doctor stood and started punching

at his iPad. "Just a minute, I'll be back."
He was. "You're right. He's got them. And he's open
til 5:30." "Okay!" I said, and stood. "How're
you gettin there?" the old guy asked.
"A cab!" I said, meaning to reassure him
that I wasn't dumb enough to waste time
waiting for a bus. He flicked a glance
toward his son who'd flicked a glance at him
the same split second. "I'll take you." "Oh,
no," I said and gestured to the old guy,
"you should stay here. A cab will come in no time."
The kid was on his feet. "His girlfriend's coming,
he'll be fine. I'll just go get the truck." "Where'd
you leave it?" asked the old guy. "Up. Above."
"Yeah," the old guy said, "you'll be a minute or two."

It was a big Dodge Ram, old, spotless.
Pitch dark and the rain had started up again,
headlights gleaming on the pavement, refracting
in the rivulets that streaked the edges of
the windshield. "Where are you going afterwards?"
he asked as we pulled in. I told him
to the ferry and insisted that I'd get
a cab. "I'll take you." "I don't know
how long I'll be." "No worries, I can wait."
When I came out, he was texting, heavy metal
screaming softly from the radio. He switched it off
as I got in. He told me, as we drove,
that he was almost finished a degree
in engineering, one term left. Thought he'd go back
in the spring if he could get his father

squared around. He'd driven truck for four years
out of high school, helped in the shop.
"Quadra," he said as he turned into the ferry
parking lot. He remembered times he'd driven there
for Timberwest, how residents had lined the roads,
yelled at him, raised their fists.
He didn't look at me. "Is someone
waiting for you on the other side?"
"I'm going to phone." He grunted
noncommittally. "You sure you'll be okay?"
"I'm sure." I pushed the big door out
against the wind, wrestled my oversize
stiff leg down to the pavement, turned.
"Bless you," I said, the door thudding against my shoulder
in the gusts. Then I stepped back,
let the wind have it, and it swung to.

HUMILITY

We find you
    in this striving, too:
        old pines

on the bluff, the plushing
    of the moss in fog.
        And in the woodsman's

naked back, the ax,
    that, glittering,
        falls with the grain.

No folded hands,
    but joy, relentless
        gratitude. You bow

to wind, to death, and
    in that gesture,
        freedom. There is nothing

that you cannot sacrifice.

SEEING

You've looked now. You've seen.
      The intricate ore,
            the charred sunlight we've bled

to feed our addictions, the seabed
      we've guttered, the soil we've enslaved
            and then raped and then forced

to bear monsters: we've broken
      what's holy. There are no
      other rivers,

no prairies, no air, no clear
      wordless root of the breath.
            No sky but the sky.

Even now, even now,
      to fail to give thanks: the same
            lethal refusal, same

turning away from the beauty
      that is. It's what
            being's made of: light

scoring the dark, dark
      marbling light. You,
            you who are weeping,

look up: it's the sky.
      And the rain that is falling
            is rain.

I took the path along the river —
July dry as late August, wanton heat — the grief
was on me hard. I sat above the falls and drowned
in noise. The shallows slipped and raced and
turned to molten glass, then loosed themselves
in heavy light-smashed froth. Here, there,
from bare rock, single harebells — six, eight inches high:
their blue flashed, hot against the grey slope
of basalt, the dense transparence of the water;
and one bent double, bobbing several seconds just above
the surface, skimming it: inside, a bee. I'd been watching
leaves — the alders dropping early in the drought —
drift, heading for the race, the sudden smoothness
as they picked up speed and then
from nowhere, in the back eddy, almost touching
the hand I'd casually dipped, another bee —
still living, one wing under, struggling
to right itself. I reached; but the current, complex,
swept it, looping further out, I reached
again, even then its body more submerged
and lost my balance, staggered, braced myself
against an offshore rock, the bee
a long way out now, caught in the main
sluice of the current, being carried frictionless
across the edge.
    Upstream, slow water
dreaming, lost, late afternoon.
The stunned boom of the falls
breachless, steady.

HAYDN: THE UNPUBLISHED SONATAS, HOB. XVI.18–20, 44–46

What are our hopes for the world?

A winter night after snow,
the long walk home, faint smudge of moon
back of the clouds; and the great weight of the firs,
the open fields whose whiteness
floats above them like a ghost.
No wind, no lamp or candle
in some distant window. You could be
the only animal. How long?
It will be hours. Only your footsteps,
and what you carry underneath your coat,
what you have folded in your arms,
what is cradled on your heart. It is so close,
maybe it's become your heart.
Perhaps it always was.

Only your footsteps, and the dark,
its nearness, and the way it does not care,
that clear, sweet silence after snow.
Is it the dark itself you love?
No. But forgive yourself for asking.

And climbing the stairs at last, then,
and lighting the fire,
and slowly, gently, taking off your coat.

The four *Ballades* of Johannes Brahms, dated 1854, were written during the period of his most intense association with Clara and Robert Schumann. In February of the same year, Robert attempted suicide and asked to be taken to an asylum for the insane. He remained there, in poor health, until his death in 1856. Soon after Robert's death, Johannes, who had been a member of the Schumann household for the period of Robert's illness, departed to live on his own. He never married and Clara did not remarry. ¶ The first page of the score of the *Ballades* bears an inscription indicating that Brahms drew inspiration from Herder's translation of the old Scottish poem "Edward." The inscription is attached to the first ballade, but the anguish that colours the plot of "Edward" seems rendered more directly in the fourth and final ballade. That ballade contains a passage of extraordinary chromatic intensity, marked "with most intimate feeling," which culminates in a stark renunciation of the key's centre. The story the music suggests is not exactly that of "Edward"; but nor is it entirely unrelated.

Consummatum est is the Latin version of the sixth of Christ's seven last words. See John 19:30.

Simplikios, a Neoplatonist of the sixth century CE, is the reason we have the core of Parmenides' argument regarding the nature of being. In his commentary on Aristotle's *Physics*, Simplikios copied out a continuous passage of some 50 lines, apologizing for appearing to be a pedant, but noting that copies of Parmenides' poem were scarce. Elsewhere in the same commentary, and in other commentaries, he copied out other shorter passages. He remains our sole source for half the surviving 150 lines of Parmenides.

My thanks to Joe Denham, to Karen Enns, and to Sue Sinclair, generous and astute readers of drafts of the manuscript. Thanks also to the editors of the journals in which some of these poems were first published: *Arc, Brick, Cyphers, The Fiddlehead, The Malahat Review, Mānoa, Prairie Fire, Prism International, Vallum,* and *The University of Toronto Quarterly.*

ALSO BY JAN ZWICKY

Poetry

Wittgenstein Elegies · 1986; 2nd ed. 2015
The New Room · 1989
Songs for Relinquishing the Earth · 1996; 2nd ed. 1998
Twenty-One Small Songs · 2000
Robinson's Crossing · 2004
Thirty-Seven Small Songs & Thirteen Silences · 2005
Forge · 2011
Chamber Music · 2015

Prose

Lyric Philosophy · 1992; 2nd ed. 2012; 2nd ed. rev. 2014
Wisdom & Metaphor · 2003; 2nd ed. 2008; 2nd ed. rev. 2014
Plato as Artist · 2009
Auden as Philosopher · 2012
The Book of Frog · 2012
Alkibiades' Love: Essays in Philosophy · 2015

Translation

Vittoria Colonna: Selections from the Rime Spirituali · 2014

Dⁿbα

Oskana Poetry & Poetics
BOOK SERIES

Publishing new and established authors, Oskana Poetry
& Poetics offers both contemporary poetry at its best
and probing discussions of poetry's cultural role.

For more information, please contact:
Karen May Clark, Acquisitions Editor
University of Regina Press
3737 Wascana Parkway
Regina, Saskatchewan S4S 0A2 Canada
karen.clark@uregina.ca